The Original Jolene:
Life Behind the Lyrics
by Jolene M. Reeves

"Not every spotlight is sought. But when it finds you,
let your truth sing."

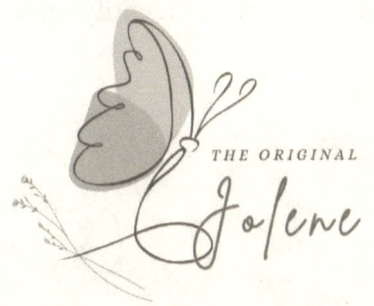

THE ORIGINAL

For permission requests, contact:
Author Contact: Jolene@theoriginaljolene.com
ISBN: 978-1-969112-00-3
Cover design by author
Printed in the United States of America
Willow & Spur Publishing
First Edition

This is a nonfiction work. Some names and identifying details may have been changed to protect privacy.

Willow & Spur

PUBLISHING

DEDICATIONS

For my Dad
Who taught me how to stir joy into Potato Soup.

You gave me grit, humor, and the kind of flour-dusted memories that never fade. Your kitchen magic, garden wisdom, and rhinoceros meat stories still feed my soul. You were the first man to believe in my spark, and I carry you in every bold sentence.

For my Mom
My best friend, my sounding board, my safe place.

You didn't always cook from scratch, but you showed me how to clean up messes with sarcasm and heart. You taught me how to face hard truths, how to laugh through chaos, and how to never apologize for being exactly who I am. I feel you with us every day and that keeps me steady.

For Rick

Though we walked different paths and spoke few words, you were part of the rhythm before the silence—a chapter in the melody of our family. May these pages carry your name with the grace of memory.

For Bennie
My co-pilot in family, farm chores, and figuring it all out mid-flight.

You always showed up. You fixed what was broken. You helped more people than anyone I know. We built a life worth keeping, and I've kept it—one pasture, one porch, and one moment at a time.

Together, you shaped my roots, my rhythm, and my reason for writing. This book carries you forward—every page, every chapter, every brave word.

Chapter List

ACKNOWLEDGMENTS

To my beautiful girls—Emma and Ally.
You are the rhythm in my soul and the reason I keep pushing forward. Thank you for your patience during emotional detours, and every moment life pulled me away from one more family dinner. You're the best chapters I've ever written.

To my family—Terri, Rick, Shirley, and every cousin, aunt, and uncle who added color, chaos, and comic relief to these pages.
Terri, your determination to reunite me with Dolly deserves its own epilogue.

To my lifelong friends—especially MaryAnne, Melissa, Camilla, and Kari. Your laughter was medicine. Your support was scaffolding. And your belief in me never once wavered. You held me together with humor, sarcasm, and soul-sister solidarity.

To Carolyn—Your gift has walked with me through seasons and stories. You were my echo when I faltered and my guide when I wandered. Thank you for being the voice beside mine, until the world finally heard.

To Tom and Alice—Thank you for teaching me how to survive and for the many things you have taught me. Best Neighbors Ever!!

To the mentors who guided me, the teachers who challenged me, and every colleague in the medical field who listened while I found my footing—Thank you for helping me stitch together my story between patient charts and coffee breaks.

I would like to acknowledge Lauren "Kat" Dufrene for her invaluable help with editing and formatting this book for me, which has been a bigger contribution than she realizes.

To every person who said, "You need to write a book."
This one's for you.

And finally, to Dolly—Whether this reaches your ears or dances gently on the edge of memory, thank you for lighting a spark that never stopped glowing. I hope we meet again, but this time, with Joleans on instead of bell bottoms and with plenty of tissues.

Introduction
The Original Jolene

Before I was Jolene, I was dancing on fireplaces and dodging bedtime.

My dad came from a large German family in Battle Creek, Michigan. Although we were living in Lansing when my mom got pregnant with me, my dad insisted on driving her to Leila Hospital in Battle Creek for the delivery—because *every* Gieske baby had been born there. Tradition trumped geography.

The Gieskes (Geese - keys) were well known in Battle Creek at that time. My great-grandfather started a butcher shop and market called *Gieske & Sons*, and every Gieske boy clocked time behind the meat counter at some point. Later on, my grandma Lorena ran a piano-style bar called *Lorena's Lounge*. There was no shortage of personality in this family.

My dad was the oldest of nine children, although two siblings passed away as infants. That left seven (five boys and two girls) all sporting names that began with "J"... except for my dad. He was Vincent, Jr., which meant everyone called him "Junior". As an adult, he *hated* being called Junior and insisted on being called Vince. Naturally, I weaponized this when he kept calling me "Tiny" well into adulthood. I'd smile sweetly and answer, "Yes, Junior." Message well received.

In 1959, my dad's youngest brother Joey passed away from leukemia just shy of his 19th birthday. It was a heartbreaking loss. Joey was the funny one, the handsome one, the one everyone adored. Those are the stories I grew up hearing, always accompanied by smiles and laughter. I remember my mom telling me Joey used to sweep the carpet with a broom because he believed it worked better than a vacuum. Funny, the details that stick with you.

My grandma Lorena came up with the name *Jolene* by blending Joey's name with my mom's—Eileene. She asked my parents to name me Jolene if I turned out to be a girl. Back in 1966, there were no ultrasounds or gender reveal parties. You crossed your fingers and waited.

My parents both loved Joey and they loved the name Jolene. So, when I arrived, my fate was sealed. They could never have imagined that one simple act—choosing a name to honor a brother and a wife—would one day inspire Dolly Parton to title one of the most iconic country ballads of all time after their youngest daughter.

Chapter 1
Tiny Ta-Go—The Sass Starts Early
Before the world knew my name, the sass knew no bounds.

As the youngest of 3 children, I was the stubborn one, the holdout at dinner who sat at the table long after everyone else had finished, refusing to eat whatever suspicious vegetable had made its way onto my plate. My dad was really hard on us for that, especially if the veggie came from *his* garden. Before I could form full sentences, I had already mastered the art of protest, particularly if my plate included anything resembling a cooked vegetable. It's no surprise that our household revolved around flavor, fire, and fierce personalities.

My dad was the head chef of our household, and not just in title. He *lived* for cooking and creating in the kitchen. Every meal was a production, and his culinary skills belonged in a magazine, not just our family dining room.

My dad's nickname for me was "Tiny Ta-Go". Cute, right? Can I tell you how much I hated that nickname? Especially if anyone outside the four walls of my house found out about it. He said I was little and fast, quick to slip away from my mom during bath time and sprint straight to the fireplace. That was my stage. I'd dance my heart out just to hear my dad laugh and postpone my bedtime. Sometimes that nickname turned into *Tiny Ta-Go-Go* when I claimed my dancing was Go-Go dancing. My mom was not thrilled. She was often frustrated with me and didn't have much patience for my nightly detour performances.

1

I was the one who questioned everything: the rules, traditions, why I had to go to bed when I clearly wasn't tired. I did not grow up with the same set of rules my siblings did. I was the "oops" baby. My parents thought they were done after the two kids. Well, the surprise was on them!

I remember one evening my dad took us to Greek Town in Detroit—his favorite spot for authentic food and a lively atmosphere. The air was brisk, probably early April, with the sun ducking down behind the buildings. As we walked from the car towards the restaurant, I saw an elderly woman nestled in a doorway, wrapped in layers, asking for money to buy a hot cup of coffee.

Without hesitation, I slipped my hand from Dad's and ran toward her—small feet on a big mission.

"Jolene Marie, get over here right now!" He called after me.

I refused to budge, pleading, "You work in a bank. You have enough money for a cup of coffee!" My stubborn heart was not backing down.

The exchange started to draw curious glances. Eventually, Dad gave me the change in his pocket, and I ran over to place it in the woman's hand. Her name was Stella, and her gratitude settled deep in my heart. On the walk back after dinner, I looked for her and she was nowhere to be seen. That night I folded her into my bedtime prayers, hoping she found warmth and a hot meal to go with her coffee.

Years later, I would look back on that chilly Detroit night and realize it was not just an act of defiance; it was something deeper. Not just because I met Stella, but because it revealed the heartbeat beneath my sass: compassion. That part of me—the part that could not ignore another person's need—was what made me different, even within my own family.

My sister and brother learned to keep the peace, fitting themselves neatly into expectations. I, on the other hand, could never ignore the fire in my chest whenever something felt unfair. That fire almost always won. I can see now why they would get so mad at me when I was continually upsetting the apple cart.

There was a significant age gap between me, my brother, and my sister: Rick was 9 years older than me, and Terri was 5 years ahead. I only remember being in school with Terri when I was very little. After my parents' divorce and the move that followed, we were never in the same school again. Most of my friends thought I was an only child—unless they came over and saw the family pictures. Maybe that is why I grew up watching everything, reading emotions, scanning for signals, and trying to make sure no one felt alone or left out.

My sister and I were very different with little resemblance to each other.

Terri has my dad's blonde hair and height. I remember always thinking how beautiful her hands were. She had long sleek hands and would paint her nails a different color every day to match her clothes, which in the 70s was very fun.

Rick was very tall and slender with brown, curly hair. When he was a teenager, I thought he looked just like Peter Frampton.

All three of us had green eyes, like my dad. None of us were lucky enough to get my mom's bright ocean blue eyes. The blue eyes may have skipped us, but we did carry something else just as powerful: the humor and the quick comebacks.

I was lucky to have *two* quick-witted parents. Somewhere along the way, I inherited their inappropriate humor genes—loud and proud. I was that kid who always wanted to sit with the grown-ups, eavesdropping like it was my part-time job. Whenever we gathered at my Grandma Gieske's house, I'd invent a dozen excuses to come upstairs from the basement just so I could soak in the adult conversations.

Even when the grown-ups tried to keep their world separate from ours, I found ways to sneak in—listening, absorbing and, of course, reporting. That instinct followed me everywhere, even through snowstorms and emergency sleepovers.

One winter, after we'd moved back to Battle Creek, a massive snowstorm knocked out our power. My grandma's house still had electricity, so my mom, Terri, and I camped there. My dad and brother stayed behind, cooking over the fireplace like they were starring in a wilderness survival show. A few other cousins piled in at Grandma's house too, turning her house into a cozy shelter. I got caught snooping on the stairs, listening to the adults talking in the kitchen. When my mom spotted me, she barked at me to get back to bed—but not before I made sure to report back to the rest of the kids all that was said about Uncle Jimmy chasing those kids who had ripped off the store at the gas station through the cemetery and scaring the crap out of them before arresting them. Gossip Girl had nothing on me.

Even as a little kid, I was often told I was an old soul. I had a knack for remembering details—crystal-clear snapshots from my earliest years. For the first six years of my life, we lived in Lansing while my dad and his Uncle Carl built our future house in Pennfield, just on the outskirts of Battle Creek. I loved visiting the construction site. The house reminded me of the house in *Gone with the Wind*. It was a stately white house with black shutters and tall white pillars on a sweeping front porch. The yard seemed gigantic before the grass and trees were planted. Across from our house sat a pond we would skate on in the winter. Behind our new backyard stretched a farm with horses and cows, and I fell head-over-heels for a little Shetland pony named Nicker. I was convinced that his name was "Dicka" and didn't learn the truth until years later. I still think my version was more fitting. He was a little troublemaker, but I adored him.

We spent lots of time in Battle Creek. My dad's entire family lived there. I never got to meet his father, my grandfather. He died of a massive heart attack when my dad was in the Army. At just 19, and as the oldest of seven kids, my dad was honorably discharged to return home and help raise his siblings. He'd been stationed at Fort Carson in Colorado at the time, and that is where he met my mom.

Fast forward to 1971 in Lansing. My favorite things were my bike and especially the Wonder Horse mounted on our swing set. I'd ride that plastic stallion for hours, pretending I was galloping across an open field. Horses have always been my spirit animal. Lucky for me, my brother and sister were too big to ride it—I had that saddle all to myself. Freedom came with squeaky springs and plastic reins.

My brother was a baseball star, and my mom was his manager, chauffeur, and biggest fan. She was usually the one going to his games and getting him to practice. One day, my dad scored tickets to a big country concert in Battle Creek. It happened to be the same day as one of my brother's games. So, my sister and I got bundled into the car with Dad for our first concert ever.

We had no idea that day would be historic—for me, for country music, and for a song that would echo across decades and change my life.

Chapter 2
Meeting Dolly—One Bell Bottom at a Time
A five-minute encounter that rewrote music legend.

When I met Dolly Parton in 1971, I had no idea I was about to become the most feared name in country music romance. I didn't have flaming locks of auburn hair or emerald eyes. My hair was more reddish brown (not fiery), and my eyes are just regular ol' green. Still, turns out those Irish genes from my mom's side were working overtime. Several years ago, my daughter begged me to do a DNA test and boom: 86% Irish. Three of my grandparents came from Germany and here I am, a walking tribute to Grandma Mary (Galloway), Irish to the core.

But I digress. At the time, I was just trying not to trip over my saddle shoes. Somehow, fate—or Dolly's brilliant mind—latched onto the name *Jolene*. She hadn't heard it before, and something about it stuck with her. She later said in an interview that she kept singing it over and over in her head until she could write it down on the tour bus.

After the song came out in 1973, my name became common knowledge. People sang it to me in bars, whispered it in checkout lines, and one boy dumped me in high school after two weeks because his mother was convinced that I was like the character Jolene in the song. No Joke.

Every time my parents introduced me to someone, the response was typically, "Oh, like the song?" And in my head, I'd groan: *Dad, please don't tell the Dolly story again.* Of course, he did. He told it more than any other story

5

in his life. Most folks believed it, some just smiled politely. But my dad? He knew, without a doubt, that our interaction with Dolly at that concert was the moment that song was crafted.

I only recently found out that he had told my stepmom Shirley the concert took place at the Ryman Auditorium in Nashville. I was stunned. I assured her—given my childhood tendency to get car sick at the *thought* of a road trip—I would not have survived a drive to Nashville. If the concert had been there, I'd have been at Rick's baseball game with my mom.

The truth? The concert was in Battle Creek, my dad's hometown, at the Kellogg Auditorium. That drive from Lansing was familiar and blessedly short. I distinctly remember the hay bales at that concert—they comforted me. We weren't very close to the stage, but the crowd was massive and, for me, overwhelming. I've always been what they call an extroverted introvert. If you know me well, you'd never guess me to be shy. Back then, surrounded by strangers, I clung to my dad's giant hand like a lifeline. At one point, I made him pick me up and carry me through the crowd just to be sure I didn't get lost.

Dad brought two record albums with us, hoping to get them signed. But instead of approaching the stage himself, he volunteered his two adorable daughters for the mission. Typical dad move.

Now, Terri and I had that classic love-hate sibling dynamic. She was the responsible one, often saddled with keeping me in line. She was also Daddy's Little Girl, the one he took fishing and trusted with his precious tools. Rick was the one he took hunting. I specialized in bathtub escapes and fireplace performances.

So, Terri and I were tasked with approaching the stage together, hand in hand. She carried the records; I just had to follow. I felt engulfed by the crowd as we walked towards the stage. All I could see were legs and it felt like people were everywhere, pushing to get to the stage first. I wanted nothing more than to get out of that tunnel of people, but the crowd had other plans. Terri and I were separated, her hand vanishing from mine, and suddenly I was surrounded by strangers with no lifeline. I panicked and started crying, fully convinced I would never find Terri or my dad ever again.

Then, out of nowhere, Dolly Parton became the hero.

From her perch on stage, she saw us getting jostled around and shouted for the crowd to "stop pushing those little girls before they get hurt." People parted, allowing us through. Dolly picked me up and brought me onto the stage while Bill Anderson helped Terri up beside me.

My dad, spotting his daughters on the stage, hustled toward us. Dolly leaned down and asked, "Where's your Mama and Daddy?"

I told her, "I don't know," still scanning for his face.

Then she asked my name.

"Jolene," I said.

She had me repeat it and asked me how I spell it. She told me she'd never heard that name before, and then she asked if my daddy's name was Joe. I was thoroughly confused—Midwestern girls aren't usually named after their dads. Why would she think that?

Finally, my dad reached us and introduced himself. He told her the story of how my grandmother made up my name, combining Uncle Joey's name and my mom's name together.

Dolly looked thoughtful. And then she said something to me that my dad never forgot and repeated often: *"Don't be surprised if one day I write a song with your name. It's just so pretty."*

And just like that, the name *Jolene* became a legend.

Chapter 3
Step Right Up
Not your average Cinderella story.

I remember the day I met Shirley at my dad's apartment in Detroit. He had never introduced us to any of his girlfriends before, so I knew this must be serious. I was nine—Terri was fourteen—and I immediately had hearts in my eyes. Terri? Not amused at all. She looked at Shirley like acknowledging her was a total betrayal to our mom. The teenage loyalty contract was strong.

Shirley was making pasta that night and invited me to help her in the kitchen. BIG WIN in my book! She asked me to hold the colander while she drained the pasta. I had never done that before, so what do you think happened when she poured the boiling hot pasta and water into the colander with my little hands holding it over the sink? Abracadabra! Pasta, GONE! Straight down the drain. When that hot steam hit my hands, I dropped it all.

I felt terrible, endlessly apologizing. She was so kind and quick to reassure me. She even took the blame, saying she didn't realize it would be too hot for me to hold onto.

She and I walked to the little market beneath the apartments to get more pasta. I thought it was super creepy, like some tunnel under the Detroit River. The apartments were old, refurbished, and full of character... and probably ghosts. Shirley whipped up a second batch of pasta, and even though Terri kept teasing me about "ruining dinner," the meal still tasted great. I remember thinking, *I really hope Dad marries her.*

Spoiler alert: He did. And to this day, Shirley is still someone I hold close. Best Bonus Mom Ever!!!

When they bought their first house (a total fixer-upper in Detroit) it had Pepto-Bismol pink cabinets and red walls. Hideous, really. My dad had a gift for seeing diamonds in the rough, a gift he passed on to me, and I'm truly grateful for that.

My first overnight stay at their house was both exciting and terrifying. I'd never stayed over without Terri, and I wasn't used to sleeping away from home. Dad's first request? Help Shirley clean out the fireplace. I genuinely thought he was joking. He wasn't. He even cracked jokes about how I hadn't yet discovered Shirley's "evil stepmother side."

Shirley made everything fun, even dirty fireplace jobs. Sometimes she'd take me to work with her at the Renaissance Center, where her office was on one of the higher floors. She hated those glass elevators. I absolutely loved them. It felt like a ride and a view all in one.

She was one of the most thoughtful, caring people I had ever met. I didn't mind helping her with things. I adored her. She always let me help her, and she taught me a lot over the years. Lessons wrapped in warmth, laughter, and pasta.

Chapter 4
Living in a Song
Being Jolene isn't just a name. It's a full-time identity.

The first time I met another person named Jolene, I was in my early 30s, attending a workshop in Los Angeles with PAX Programs. She was from somewhere in the Pacific Northwest—Seattle, or maybe Portland—and I remember being so weirded out. I hadn't realized how much I was used to being the only Jolene. My name had always felt one-of-a-kind, and I relished the fact that my favorite grandma had made it up. Other friends had names so common their teachers had to call them by their last name just to clarify who they were talking to. I'm guessing it is like being in a store where someone shouts "Mom!" and half the women turn around. I have never had that happen with my name though.

In third grade, a girl named Jileen moved into my apartment complex... and into my classroom. At first, I thought that our names being similar was so cool. That was until kids started calling her Jolene and me Jileen. That novelty wore off fast. Thankfully, she preferred "Jil", which kept me safe in my name bubble. Jil and I became close friends, inseparable for two years. When her family moved to Bloomfield Hills, we tried to stay in touch; but life drifted on, as it does when you're too young to manage long-distance friendship with only a landline.

Years later, a girl named Joelle came to town during my sophomore year of high school. For reasons I still don't understand, we never liked each other.

Maybe it was the name thing—too similar to mine, but not quite. We were both frustrated when people would call her Jolene and me Joelle. We shared mutual friends but never exchanged many words, even at our 20th and 40th reunions. Funny how things turn out sometimes.

The most surreal encounter came decades later, in a PACU unit at a hospital in Greenville, South Carolina. I was there with my goddaughter, Jeniffer, for a procedure, and her nurse introduced herself: "Hi, I'm Jolene." Spelled exactly the same. We only exchanged polite smiles. A couple of hours in, she finally asked me where my name came from. I didn't tell the Dolly story—even though I could feel her husband, Hugo, hoping I would. I shared that my grandma invented it by combining two family names. She said her mother named her after a childhood best friend. And you know what I forgot to ask? *Who was her mother? Where did she grow up? What if I was that friend?* I'm still considering tracking her down, just to find out. I was so focused on Jeniffer, I didn't think of it until I was driving back to Atlanta.

Over almost six decades, I've only had four notable name encounters. That might be strange for most people but, for me, it was oddly validating. My name was mine. Most folks share names with hundreds, thousands, millions. I never had that experience.

But of course, there's *the* name connection everyone wonders about. Some people mention it immediately when they meet me. Others wait, awkwardly, before blurting out, "So... were you named after that song?"

And that's when I explain the backstory—or not. When I posted my story for the first time on social media, tons of people reached out saying, "How did I not know this about you?" Well, let me tell you.

Until Dolly's first book came out in 1994—when I was 28—I wasn't even convinced that she was talking about *me*. I figured the song could've been written about some other Jolene. After all, I couldn't be the only one, could I? My sister Terri called me, shouting about a passage Dolly had written describing this little girl from Michigan with red ponytails and green eyes that she named the song after. She mailed me the book with a sticky note on the page so I could see it for myself. I remember her words clear as day: "Holy shit—after all these years, Dad was right!"

Dad *loved* telling that story. And he was known for his storytelling. There was always a thread of truth, but let's just say the fish got bigger with every retelling. Like the version where we supposedly met Dolly at the Ryman Auditorium in Nashville—my stepmom Shirley believed that one. But that's how it goes. How big was that fish, Dad?

So, why did I keep this quiet for so long?

Well, at first, I wasn't really sure it was the truth. My dad never wavered, but I needed something solid. Second, and this is big, I was a busty girl—DDs in junior high school, bigger after breastfeeding my two girls. And do you know how many people sang that song to me? I'd hear, "Jolene, please don't take my man!" at school, parties, gas stations, you name it. Mostly people just sang the main chorus: "Jolene, Jolene, Jolene, Joleeeeene..."

If you met my dad, you knew the story. I would ask my friends not to share it. I was already shy (remember—extroverted introvert) and I didn't need more attention drawn to me from a song about a woman flirting with a married man. I didn't like being reduced to lyrics I didn't write, for a moment I didn't control. That song cast a long shadow for a long time.

Now, here's the truth: I never disliked the song itself; I disliked how it made me feel growing up. I'd constantly wonder, *Why did she have to be a tramp?* That was my name, after all. And yet, people expected me to love the attention, to shout the story from every rooftop. As an adult, I've shared that discomfort with those who couldn't quite grasp why I wasn't celebrating it. When I explain that the character of Jolene wasn't exactly the hero of the story, I often hear, *"She wasn't doing anything wrong. She was just a beautiful woman being flirtatious. She didn't steal anyone."* Honestly, that's been surprisingly comforting to me. In my head was the fear of a little girl that didn't want the attention drawn to her.

Growing up as Jolene wasn't just about dodging Dolly references. It was about navigating real danger, real fear, and real moments that shaped who I have become.

While some kids worried about spelling tests and recess drama, I was busy escaping a serial killer.

Chapter 5
Did that really happen?
How many people can say they escaped a serial killer?

In 1977, we lived in an apartment complex in Southfield, Michigan (post-divorce). Our building was at the very back of the complex, and we had two ways to get home from school: walk the long, winding road back or take a shortcut along a grassy strip behind several buildings. On one side was a wooded area with a chain-link fence and on the other, the backside of 4 apartment buildings.

I remember snow mounds still edging the ground on this sunny day in early April 1977. My friend Debbie and I turned onto the shortcut after passing the apartment manager's office. Debbie was chatting away as usual. I wasn't really listening, because I saw a man walk around the first building and then toward us. He was wearing jeans and a faded flannel shirt under a jean jacket. His greasy hair hung down by his thick, long sideburns. Something bulky glinted on his wrist—maybe a watch or bracelet.

He didn't move aside to let us pass. Instead, *we* moved to avoid *him*. That's when he grabbed both of us—right in the crotch. I jumped back. He turned on Debbie, who erupted like a firecracker, kicking, flailing, and screaming. I was frozen in place, screaming and backing away. She looked like the Tasmanian Devil from Saturday morning cartoons.

We made so much noise that someone was bound to hear us. He knew it too. He let go, bolted toward 12 Mile Road, leapt over the short brick wall, and disappeared.

We ran all the way home, still screaming as we passed three long buildings. When we burst through the door, my sister Terri—already in high school—was there. She immediately called the police and then my mom at work.

We had no idea who he was yet, but we quickly learned.

After the investigation, we discovered that Julie—the apartment manager's daughter and one of Terri's friends—had seen the man before we got off the bus that day. She noticed a blue Gremlin parked on the dirt road across 12 Mile. The news had reported that the Oakland County Child Killer was likely driving a blue Gremlin. Julie thought he looked like the sketch from the newspaper, so she left the window to find it. When she came back with the paper in her hand, he was gone, though the blue Gremlin was still on the dirt road.

When I saw that sketch from the newspaper, I screamed, "That's him! That's the guy who grabbed us!"

The police dog tracked his scent exactly where we said he'd walked and where he'd jumped the wall. It was all there.

Still... the police didn't believe us.

They separated Debbie and me during questioning. Our stories didn't align perfectly. They said I had *too much* detail, and that Debbie's description didn't quite match mine. I was furious. I had been focused on him the entire time he approached us. Debbie was mid-story, barely noticing him until it happened. Didn't they appreciate my photographic memory?

My mom started to doubt us, too. She thought we might've made it up for attention. That stung. Julie saw him! The dog tracked him! *Why don't you believe us?*

For a month, Debbie's mom drove us to and from school. We stuck to the main roads and never walked home alone again. Another close friend, MaryAnne, was home with chicken pox when it all happened. She was devastated. She begged her dad to let her come visit, just to hug us and make sure we were okay. The entire experience had shaken all of us—kids navigating fear in a time when safety felt stolen. It was a terrifying chapter, and we were just trying to find peace in our small world again.

Years later, in my mid-20s, when I was visiting my mom and Terri in Michigan, I brought it up—finally. My mom was shocked, apologetic, tears in her eyes. She said she never realized how real it was, just that our stories confused the police and it was easier to believe it wasn't true. She hugged me tight and said, "I can't believe my baby was attacked by a serial killer." That moment was a release. I tucked that memory deep in my brain after that.

Fast forward to 2008. I'm married, living in Louisville, KY. Bennie's working late at the VA. The kids are playing in the other room, and I've got the TV on as I'm tidying up. A rerun of *America's Most Wanted* comes on. The segment features the Oakland County Child Killer—and I freeze.

I scream, "OH MY GOD!" It all came rushing back to me. I called Bennie at work and blurted out everything. He was shocked that I could bury that so deep.

Years later, I reconnected with Debbie after three decades. When I thanked her for saving our lives, she went quiet. She had buried it, too. That moment flooded back for both of us.

It's strange how our brains protect us. Burying trauma in the vault until something—a voice, a sketch, a rerun—unlocks it.

Looking back, it's incredible how moments that happen in mere seconds can shape your entire sense of safety as well as memory. For weeks, life felt different. We clung to routines, held hands tighter, took fewer shortcuts. Even our friend MaryAnne, stuck at home in quarantine, was heartbroken that she couldn't be there for us. She begged her dad to let her visit just to hug us, to make it all feel better. That simple act—her worry—meant the world.

For years, that memory stayed tucked in a quiet drawer in my mind. Not forgotten. Just folded away.

Sometimes, life gives you a story that no one believes at first. Sometimes, it takes time—decades even—for the truth to feel safe enough to resurface. But whether it was the sound of our screaming, the flash of a greasy jean jacket in the snow, or the comforting hug from my mom years later, it all became part of my story, a story not just of fear but of courage... and survival.

(A copy of the newspaper article that shows the sketch that most resembled the man that attacked us.)

Chapter 6
The Silver Lining Still Shines
Because even the darkest memories can reveal light.

When I think back to high school, it's a mixed bag: some glittering, golden memories and a few I've worked hard to heal from. I'm the kind of person who doesn't linger in the bad. I sift through it gently, looking for the lessons and the silver lining. I might not see the silver lining right away, but I never lose sight of finding value in the worst circumstances.

I couldn't go anywhere in school without someone singing my name. Sometimes it was classmates, sometimes even teachers, calling me out with *that* song. I'd smile and humor them, waiting for it to end, while thinking, *Why me?* I never liked that kind of public attention. Still, I loved having a unique name in the sea of Jennifers, Lisas, and Kims. There was no question who they were talking about. It was always me. That was both a blessing and a trap. Let's just say, I couldn't sneak around much being *the only Jolene* in my little corner of the world.

I was mostly a good kid—no lies, no sneaking (well, maybe once, and we all got caught), always the designated driver in my giant '72 Ford LTD. I wasn't a drinker after what happened in my freshman year. I even practiced quarter bounce at home (with water) so I'd never be forced to down a beer. Carbonated drinks still aren't my thing, and alcohol just wasn't part of my story. A big reason? My mom was a pretty serious alcoholic during my junior high and high school years. Not the fun kind. The mean kind.

There's only one high school memory I'd call truly horrific, which is the other reason I am not a big drinker.

I was a freshman. A really good friend—two years older—threw a party while her parents were out of town. Mad Dog 20/20 and Boone's Farm flowed like a fountain. I'd never had a drink before, so naturally, I grabbed the purple bottle of MD 20/20. Purple was my favorite color. That night, it didn't take much for me to get drunk, and I passed out in her brother's bedroom.

A sophomore boy from the basketball team decided that my unconscious body meant consent. He took something that wasn't his to take. I woke up disoriented, bleeding, pants gone, and terrified. I yelled, and he shrugged from the doorway, "Oh come on, you know you liked it." That sentence cut deeper than any physical pain.

I remember stumbling through the house, dazed, crying, trying to find someone who could make it make sense. The first person I saw was a guy I'd had a crush on for years. His look of disgust shattered me. He thought I'd chosen this. That moment wrecked me.

A friend of that *sophomore boy* eventually told him to leave, bless him. I stayed behind with the rest of the party crowd, trying to hold it together, but something in me broke. That night something sacred was stolen from me. I wasn't necessarily waiting for marriage, but I *was* waiting for love. And choice. That mattered.

Years of therapy helped me process it. I've done courses, healing work, and soul work, but trauma has a sneaky way of lingering. Just when you think you've got a grip on it, you log into Facebook and see *his* face under *People You May Know*. That happened a few years ago, right before the 40th reunion. My breath vanished. Panic surged like I was 14 again.

I've only been to two reunions—my 20th, when I was pregnant with my youngest daughter, and my 40th. So many people I hadn't seen in decades showed up, and it was heartwarming. It also made me homesick for lake life and face-to-face connections. Social media helps us stay in the loop, but a ten-minute reunion conversation can't replace real, quality time.

I realized something about high school: it's just happenstance. There are people I've gotten close to as adults who went to school with me, yet we never connected back then. And now? I wish we had. It feels like I missed out on some special friendships.

During the 40th reunion, I kept watching for that sophomore boy (now a man), worried he might show up. Our class has always included the class of '83, and, truthfully, my junior year (when they were seniors) was my best. Most of my favorite people were in that class. Thankfully, he wasn't there. I did get to see a few of my very favorite people, which was healing and helped dissipate the fear I was feeling from being away from my hometown for so long.

And there's that one man in particular... my high school crush from the class of '83. Seeing him again was the highlight of my trip. If I had to pick one person to spend more time with, it would be him. I still hold out hope that life may surprise us both with a second chance one day. A girl can dream.

Chapter 7
Gieske Tales and Kitchen Magic
Where culinary brilliance meets stubborn toddler defiance.

I'll never forget the year *Grandma Got Runover by a Reindeer* was popular in the early 80s. Every Thanksgiving, we would head to my Grandma Gieske's house in Battle Creek for dinner. That year, she'd already started decorating for Christmas—especially the Styrofoam wall display of Santa and his reindeer, flying proud above the couch.

On the way there, Dad kept raving about the song, laughing like he'd just discovered comedy. The moment we arrived, he slipped into Grandma's bathroom with a pair of scissors. His plan? Snip a lock of hair to tape onto Rudolph's hoof—proof of the crime scene. I exclaimed a big fat, "NO WAY." Nobody touched my hair. I told him to use Terri's hair since hers matched Grandma's more anyway. Terri was blonde like Dad. I was redheaded defiance in a holiday sweater.

He pulled it off and waited for the song to come on the radio. When it did, he cranked it, marched Grandma over to the wall, and pointed to Rudolph's hoof. "THAT's the one that got you!" He cackled. None of us had seen him tape the hair to the Styrofoam hoof. Grandma thought it was silly. Everyone else thought it was hilarious.

To this day, I make two dishes every Thanksgiving: her sage stuffing and her cranberry sauce. Dad taught me both. We'd stale real bread, chop everything by hand—none of that bagged stuff. She wasn't big on kitchen help, especially with a house full of grandkids, but I always feel like she's right there with me when I cook those dishes.

Dad's love of food came from his grandma, the original Gieske matriarch. He spent summers on her farm, an escape from the chaos of his own house and siblings. From her, he learned to make German potato soup, sauerkraut & sausage, potato pancakes, and egg noodles from scratch. They'd hang all over the kitchen, drying like edible garlands.

Me, Terri, and Mom had a bad habit of sneaking the dough. Terri was the distraction queen. We'd send her in to find Dad and keep him busy while I swiped some noodles for us. If he caught wind of it, you'd hear him yell, "Tiny Ta-Go!! GET IN HERE!" I'd try to play innocent, but the flour on my face and shirt always gave me away.

"I wasn't the only one!" I'd protest.

Technically true. But also, technically obvious. He knew I was the instigator.

Every Sunday there was a proper sit-down meal. One night, Dad made a big pot roast, and Rick told me we were eating the neighbor's cow, Mable.

"WHAT?! Pot roast is cow meat??" I stormed outside to look for her. I didn't see her anywhere. I also didn't eat another bite of that roast.

Rick thought this was hilarious, but my parents were less than thrilled. From then on, I refused to eat any meat without interrogating its backstory: "What type of animal is this?" "Where did it come from?" "Did it have a name?"

The next week, my dad made a big chicken dinner with potatoes and corn.

"I'm not eating chicken anymore," I declared.

He looked me dead in the eye. "It's not chicken, Tiny. It's pheasant."

"Pheasant?" I asked. "What is a pheasant?"

"It's *not* a farm animal," he tells me.

"Hmmmm... OK, I'll try it."

I'm *quite* sure he had a serious chat with Rick to keep his mouth shut about where food comes from.

The next time he made pot roast, he prepared me upfront. "We're having rhinoceros meat for dinner tonight."

I was very skeptical. I chewed cautiously. Turns out, I *loved* rhinoceros' meat and asked for it often.

In my mid-twenties, I asked my dad to send me his greatest hits—recipes I'd grown up loving—because I was starting a family cookbook. He sent several, including the German potato soup, Grandma's stuffing, and her cranberry sauce. The last one in the bunch had an interesting title, in his handwriting: **RHINOCEROS MEAT**. I still have these recipes today in a special place and

21

I enjoy pulling them out to see his writing and have a laugh.

I've talked a lot about my dad—his kitchen wizardry, his flour-dusted drama—but let me tell you a secret about my mom. She was a terrible cook. Truly. There was only *one* thing she made from scratch that I absolutely loved: her baked chicken wings. I've recreated them countless times, clinging to the one recipe she owned with pride.

Her idea of cooking? Read the box. Read the can. Heat and serve. My mom had grown up very poor, one of five siblings (though one sister tragically passed away as an infant), and her big rule was that food was not to be wasted, *ever*. She'd scold, "There are kids starving in Bangladesh!"

I'd respond, "Then you can mail my leftovers to them!"

Not her favorite comeback, but she heard it often. She was taught that you clean your plate, no exceptions. I was that exception. It would drive her nuts, and she would often eat the food remaining on my plate.

One night, Dad had to work late at the bank, or so Mom thought. Turns out that he came home earlier than expected and walked into what he clearly considered a horror film. The scene? All of us lined up in the living room, perched on folding TV trays, devouring TV dinners while watching the television.

He was aghast. Outraged. Mortified. We were thrilled. The Salisbury steak was questionable, but the rebellion tasted amazing. He looked like he might have had a stroke right there. His homemade meals were sacred, and processed food was blasphemy. We just quietly giggled through our gravy, blaming mom.

Food wasn't just fuel in the Gieske house; it was art, storytelling, and a vehicle for passing down great recipes and sly humor. It fed our bellies, yes, but also our boldness. Between noodle heists and Thanksgiving prank wars, I learned that food had rhythm, reverence, and rebellion. The kitchen was a stage, and Dad was the headliner. The smells, the scoldings, the floury face smirks—they all live rent-free in my memories.

Even now, when I make Grandma's stuffing or Dad's tabouleh, it's like they're standing beside me—one with a wooden spoon, the other probably plotting another rhinoceros roast reveal.

The magic wasn't just in the recipes. It was in the resilience they baked into me. The stubborn toddler who refused pot roast and chicken now leads with grit and grace, and she still asks far too many questions at dinner, always interested in how things are made.

Between Grandma's feisty presence, Dad's culinary theatrics, and Mom's creative use of the frozen food aisle, our kitchen was never dull. We might've had hot dogs one night and rhinoceros meat the next, but every meal told a story and usually involved a laugh, a tug-of-war over control, and at least one battle cry of "Tiny Ta-Go!"

To this day, I can say that I have never eaten a pea on my plate.

Even now, when I cook those cherished recipes or catch myself improvising in the kitchen, I feel all of them with me. Not just the flavors—but the voices, the quirks, the lessons, and the love. The magic was never in the ingredients alone. It lived in the characters who stirred them.

Chapter 8
Unscheduled, Undeniable
Because sometimes the best arrivals don't follow a plan.

My mom and dad were finally stepping into a sweet spot in life. Terri was about to start kindergarten (no pre-school back then), and both kids would soon be out of the house during the day. Mom was eyeing some well-earned breathing room. Freedom. A few glorious hours without childcare.

So much for that plan. Surprise! Here comes Jolene!

My childhood looked very different from Rick's and Terri's. They were close in age and, for a time, each other's built-in playmates. Me? I had solo mornings with Mom while they were off at school. I had a front-row seat to her humor, her quirks, and the deep sighs that said, *I love you... but please go play by yourself now.*

One of Rick and Terri's favorite complaints growing up was, "You never let us do that at her age!" Hard to argue. I was the youngest and, according to sibling law, that meant I got away with everything. I can remember that I always thought it was interesting how regimented my brother was at dinner. He ate everything on his plate and didn't touch his milk until his food was gone. I thought that was so weird.

Rick and Terri were often tasked with watching me, though neither was ever thrilled about it. Rick was a terrible babysitter. He preferred playing his bass guitar alone in his room. Every time I hear "Deep Purple", I picture him jamming out to that iconic riff. Terri was more attentive, but not much happier about the job.

One year, my parents asked Terri what she wanted for her birthday. Her request? *Dinner alone with them at a restaurant. No Rick, No Jolene.*

I sensed something was off all day. Everyone was acting weird and secretive. The vibe was definitely off. Then suddenly, the three of them vanished. I searched the house and finally asked Rick where they went.

He looked me dead in the eye. "They moved to Wisconsin and left you with me."

WHAT?! "You're lying!"

"Then why didn't they say goodbye?" He teased. "You know Terri's their favorite. Are any of her clothes missing? Where are the suitcases?"

I melted down. Full, major meltdown. It felt like they were gone forever. When they came home, I let them have it. "You're so mean! You snuck out and left me with Rick! He didn't do anything with me!"

After that, they promised no more sneaky exits, but only if I could handle hearing the truth without tantrums. Eye roll... *Okay.* (My mom was never a fan of the eye roll.)

Despite my dramatics, one of the things my mom adored about me was how well I entertained myself. Hours could pass with me lost in my own world. I still cherish alone time today. It's what keeps me grounded.

Terri had her classic middle-child moments. We'd hold coloring contests and Rick always picked me as the winner, solely to drive her crazy. Why do you think I suggested the contest? Terri would explode. "She can't even color inside the lines! Hers is not better than mine... ***MOM!!!***"

Rick tortured Terri much more than me. I think my age gave me diplomatic immunity. Let's be honest here, tormenting the middle child is practically a sibling requirement.

One of Rick's favorite pranks involved Dad's old Army gas mask. He'd slip outside in the dark, crouch by a window, and just wait. The first time I saw that freaky creature staring in at us, I screamed so hard I nearly passed out. In my mind, it wasn't Rick. It was the Grim Reaper coming to get us.

Speaking of passing out...

One day during a toddler tantrum with Terri, I held my breath so long I dropped like a stone. Terri was horrified. *She'd killed her baby sister!* She screamed for Mom and, suddenly, she was my new hero. She gave me everything I wanted, avoided any conflict, and did her best not to upset me. MAJOR WIN.

And guess what that taught me? This trick worked *every time.*

My parents grew worried. They thought I was doing it for attention, so they called the pediatrician to get some advice. He told them to ignore me, that I'd start breathing again on my own as soon as I passed out. And he was right. Once the attention disappeared, so did my flair for the dramatic. It took Terri a little longer not to be hooked by it, but eventually even she stopped falling for it. The gig was up. The party was over.

Of course, Christmas had its own brand of magic at our house. Dad and Rick would grab a ladder, climb onto the roof, and go full production mode with Dad shouting "Ho Ho Ho!" in a deep voice into the cold night while Rick shook jingle bells like his life depended on it.

"Terri! Santa is on our roof!!" I was breathless with joy, sure that any movement or sound from me might scare him off. Still... I couldn't help listening for just one more footstep or one more sleigh bell.

I was given the nickname "the blab" by my sister and brother because I could not keep a secret, especially around Christmas presents. When I was about 3 ½ years old, my dad kept making comments to us kids on Christmas eve. "I wonder what's in this box?" The tag read *'To Daddy from Ricky, Terri, and Jolene'*. It was a smaller box, and he kept trying to guess silly things, asking, "Is it a hammer?" He picked me up and asked me to give him a hint.

Terri was giving me major side-eye, telling me, "Don't tell him!!"

I looked right at him and said, "Daddy, you remind me of a cuff link!"

My dad thought that was hilarious, while my mom, Rick, and Terri were glaring at me for giving it away—again!

For those of you old enough to remember record albums, it was always a joke because it was so obvious when there was a record album wrapped under the tree. One year when I was a bit older—maybe 3rd of 4th grade—we were all at the dinner table with my mom at the apartment, and Terri said, "Gee, I wonder what that one is, Rick?" It was one of Rick's presents she was pointing at—obviously a record album.

I spout out, "Oh, you mean the Alice Cooper record next to his basketball?"

The family tried really hard to make sure I was not around to see presents being bought or wrapped—birthday, Christmas, whatever the reason. Everyone knew not to let Jolene know what it was. This is where the saying "Honest to a fault" comes into play for me. Luckily, I grew out of that blab phase by the time I hit junior high.

Being the "oops baby" didn't make me an afterthought; it made me unforgettable. I arrived right when they thought the parenting chapter was winding down and rewrote the ending with glitter, sass, and an unshakeable sense of wonder. I lived with only child energy in a house full of stories, mischief, and gas masks at the window. I didn't just grow up. I grew into myself, one independent daydream at a time.

And looking back, I know now: unplanned doesn't mean unwanted. It means the universe made space for a wild card—for the girl who refused pot roast, started coloring contests she couldn't win, and still believes in rooftop reindeer.

Chapter 9
Married, Mothered & Mended
Marriage, motherhood, career—and the ache that changed everything.

Turning thirty felt like such a letdown. I remember that ache vividly—how it seemed like life was passing me by. I had a great career, sure, but no husband, no children, and no clear path to the family life I'd always dreamed of.

So, I made myself a quiet promise: *If I don't get married in time to have children, I'll become an elementary school teacher.* Children were non-negotiable for me. I babysat them, pet-sat their families, house-sat their homes—I couldn't imagine a life without little ones in it. If I couldn't have children of my own, I'd surround myself with others.

I decided to spend my early thirties working on me.

Therapy originally began at 23, at the urging of the first doctor I worked for in South Miami. She saw right through me—saw things I couldn't or wouldn't. At the time, I was engaged to a much older Argentinian man, and completely miserable. She knew I was chasing security and not joy. That was my pattern. I believed that men my age were immature, so I chose older partners and shrank inside relationships that made me smaller.

Everything shifted when I met Dr. Gershman. I was working in finance at Expressway Toyota, and her husband worked in leasing. She visited often and got to know me—and eventually told me I was too good to be stuck at that dealership. She offered me a chance to train as a medical assistant. I quit my job with Toyota and leapt into medicine. I never looked back.

From medical assisting to the front office, I found my lane. I loved the insurance work, the patient care, and the office management, even more so because I understood both sides of the practice. It was a calling I hadn't expected and deeply needed.

I didn't just work on my career; I worked on my soul.

At 31 I enrolled in the Landmark Forum and followed it with courses that broke open my self-awareness. I left victimhood behind, gave up "reasons", and started owning every part of my life. I stopped settling. I stopped apologizing. And most importantly, I stopped disappearing in relationships. I found my strength, my power, and my transformation.

Landmark led me to PAX Programs, Inc., and Alison Armstrong's transformational work. After attending the *Celebrating Men, Satisfying Women* workshop, I was hooked. I trained to be a workshop manager, led events in Atlanta, traveled to New York and L.A., and eventually became an introductory workshop leader. I was *all in*. The camaraderie was electric—the women, the conversations, and the Men's Panels (don't get me started on the Men's Panels). It was a time of expansion, healing, and clarity.

Two weeks after taking the *Understanding Men & Marriage* course in New York, I met my future husband.

We'd spoken on the phone several times before we met—he reached out through my old Matchmaker.com account, which I thought I had deactivated. My dad passed away the July before, and I'd spent the holidays in Michigan grieving and recalibrating. I postponed meeting Bennie until late January.

When we finally met, the sparks flew.

He greeted me with flowers, opened every door, pulled out my chair, and we talked for hours. I was smitten with his charm and drawn to his spirit. He was serving in the Army National Guard and talked about flying airplanes with a vibrant light in his eyes. He was a private pilot, and aviation was his soul's home.

We dated for thirteen months before he proposed at Ray's on the River in Atlanta. Then came marriage, pregnancy, and a whirlwind of joy—and worry.

During my first OB visit (in the same practice I worked in), a large thyroid tumor was discovered. I dropped weight rapidly and had to make a difficult decision. I chose to have surgery mid-pregnancy instead of waiting until after I delivered. I wanted to be able to breastfeed my daughter and knew delaying would risk that. I was surrounded by brilliant doctors and midwives, and I leaned into that support with deep gratitude.

One of the most rewarding things I've done in my life is being the mom to my 2 girls. We moved to Michigan when our girls were two and five—into the same neighborhood I'd lived in growing up, near Wolverine Lake. It felt like coming home. They took their first horseback riding lessons in Milford, and I reveled in winter's embrace. I've always loved the cold weather and snow, and the magic it brings.

Bennie, on the other hand, was less enchanted. After one brutal winter, he asked to move back to Georgia. I understood since he hadn't grown up with snowstorms or icy driveways. His family traveled the world with the Air Force before settling in Dayton, Ohio.

So, we bought a small three-acre farm in Suwanee, Georgia. We raised our daughters, rescued horses, dogs, and cats, and built a life on a front porch overlooking a grazing pasture. It was everything I'd dreamed of as a little girl: husband, children, animals, nature, love.

We were the average family, working hard, building something solid, raising kids with laughter and expectations. In March 2020, we finally bought our first Ford F-150, a moment that felt like arrival. Three days later, the world shut down.

Both Bennie and I already had home-office flexibility, so we adapted quickly to the quarantine. We set up separate workspaces and dug in. Our jobs didn't change—just the location. Five days a week, we were now co-working partners. The girls, in high school, shifted to virtual classes. One a freshman, one a junior.

Oddly enough, we grew closer as a family—more dinners together, more game nights. It wasn't all bad. I knew people who were really struggling, but inside our four walls, quarantine felt like survival as well as connection.

I was scheduled to have surgery at the end of March 2020 and that was cancelled. Only critical surgeries were kept on the schedule. I was having the other half of my thyroid removed for another large mass that was pushing everything over onto my vocal cords. My voice had changed, and I was struggling to sing—which I LOVED to do, especially in my car. Although I played the flute from 4th grade through 12th grade, the music venue I relished was singing. I had an amazing choir teacher in high school who was truly a mentor for me in many ways (Thank you, Gary Weidenaar!). I knew I was never going to have any type of career from singing. I just loved it and missed it.

My surgery was rescheduled to the end of May and my amazing surgeon, Dr. Garcha, did all he could to save that vocal cord. He told me in post-op that the mass had grown and was much bigger than he expected. He told us it was a "mess" in there to clear out. He referred me back to see my ENT, Dr. Robb, as it could take 6 months to a year for a paralyzed vocal cord to "wake-up". (I am so grateful to these two amazing doctors.)

Dr. Garcha did my original thyroid removal in 2003. He honestly could have been a plastic surgeon and I am grateful he did not pursue that path. After two surgeries, you still cannot see my scar unless you are really looking for it.

Bennie really liked Dr. Garcha. They were both private pilots, so they had a special respect and camaraderie for each other.

When school started in August 2020, both girls caught COVID-19. First Emma and then Ally. Thank God both girls had mild symptoms, though still terrifying. Emma got Covid first and was quarantined in her room. Bennie would take food into her in full Hazmat style. He was covered from head to toe in anything he could find – oven mitts on his hands, two aprons on, a towel on his bald head like a sheik, big goggles, and several masks on. He looked ridiculous... and yet it made Emma laugh.

By the end of September, it was our turn; and Bennie and I got slammed, quite the opposite of mild symptoms.

I have never felt so awful for so long. Every movement was an effort. Someone had suggested we check our temperatures regularly and buy a pulse oximeter to ensure our oxygen levels were above 90. Bennie was clearly struggling. His oxygen levels kept dipping. When the pulse ox hit 89, I loaded him into the truck and drove him to the Emergency Room, even though I could barely keep myself upright. I remember having thoughts that we might not survive. It had been over a week, and we were still dangerously sick.

I could not go into the ER with him and, after several hours, they checked him out and sent him *home* with an oxygen tank. I couldn't believe it. I drove back to the ER to pick him up.

I set up the oxygen tank, and we both hit the bed again. I monitored his O2 levels, and they kept dropping. I felt so much guilt that the two of us were so sick—so grateful our kids were old enough to take care of themselves, the house, and all the animals.

The next morning, Bennie's oxygen level was down to 84 with the oxygen mask on. I rushed him back to the ER. The same ER doctor was still on shift. He saw Bennie walking in and knew instantly. *This was bad.* He apologized for sending him home the day before and admitted him.

Bennie insisted I get looked at too. We were placed in separate areas of the ER and that was the last time I saw my conscious husband.

He was admitted to the step-down ICU, and I was sent home. We could talk by phone, though I wasn't allowed to visit him. His condition deteriorated over the next week and eventually he was moved to the ICU. After four weeks, they called me. It was a Friday. The doctor told me that he had to intubate Bennie and that I should come to the hospital to see him. Suddenly, *now* I was allowed to visit.

I was so frustrated and furious.

"Now? NOW you let me see him, when he won't even know I'm there?"

I left immediately. Of course I did. I was desperate to see him after so long and yet scared to see him. I had not seen him in a month.

What I saw broke me. My clean-cut, "inspection ready" husband—always shaved, always sharp—was pale, disheveled, and fading. He looked like a man with no spirit, already halfway gone with his body lifeless.

Bennie spent seven weeks in that hospital before he passed away.

He was too young. It didn't seem real. I couldn't even say the word "died" for over a year. It was too final. Too cruel. That entire first year is a blur—one long, aching breath. I did everything I could to keep the girls grounded... to make things feel *normal*... even when nothing was normal. My oldest was a senior in high school. She kept saying, "He won't see me graduate... He won't walk me down the aisle..." And my youngest, his little Bug, was heartbreak wrapped in silence.

We all grieved differently, but we were grieving together, walking this path we didn't want to be on. We had a beautiful service for him at our church. Bert and his Army buddy, Frank, gave amazing eulogies. So many people came to say good-bye and support the girls and me. The military funeral was the hardest for me—listening to that 21-gun salute and receiving the flag off his casket. It was so surreal. How did we get here? I felt like a zombie, going through the motions and not knowing what I was doing at the same time. I remember Dr. Patterson hugging me, and I could see my girls crying over her shoulder. My heart was broken in pieces for us. How were we going to survive this?

I would never have survived that time without my family, my friends, and my church family. They carried me when I couldn't carry myself. They reminded me that love doesn't vanish; it just changes shape. I had to keep my faith, knowing we would survive this... somehow... someway. It is no joke when they say, "it takes a village." It really does. I could not be more grateful for my village.

We didn't have a perfect life. We had a *real* one. Being married to Bennie was built on laughter, teamwork, and the kind of quiet gestures that never made it to social media but carried everything that mattered. We had our arguments, sure, but we never lost sight of us. He was my best friend. He showed up in little ways and big ones: silly nicknames, taking care of the animals with vigor, and drawing me a bath when the kids pushed every button I had. He had this way of making me feel like I was not alone. He had my back.

Motherhood changed everything. Overnight, I went from wife to CEO of Chaos Management. Two daughters, full hearts, constant noise. They tested me, inspired me, cracked me open, and taught me how deep love could go. I wasn't always graceful. I've burned dinners, twisted my ankle, showed up in yesterday's mascara—but I was *in it*. Fully and fiercely ALL IN.

Work was always more than a paycheck. I was living proof that the Midwest Work Ethic was a real thing. I could do hard things, chase goals, lead teams, and keep the lights on when everything else felt shaky. Balancing career and family was not a walk in the park; it was a bucking Bronco. Somehow, we kept the rhythm going. We figured things out.

And then, that rhythm stopped. The other half of us was missing.

When Bennie died, it felt like someone pulled the plug on the music. Everything went dark and quiet. I had to rediscover how to move, speak, and *be* without him. Who was I now? Somehow... I kept putting one foot in front of the other—not perfectly, not always with a smile, but always with heart and faith.

Love didn't leave. It shifted. It wrapped around my girls and held us in the worst moments. It showed up in casseroles from neighbors, text check-ins from friends, and sleepy hugs that said, *I'm still here. We're still us.*

And now? I keep building—not the life I thought I'd have, but the one I'm proud to carry forward. Bennie deserves a legacy. My daughters deserve stability. And I deserve joy again when it's ready to meet me.

I know Bennie watches over us. Every time I hear a single engine airplane in the sky, I think of him and know he will make sure we are happy and taken care of.

Chapter 10
Hot Glue, Healing & Whole Foods

It's amazing what a craft aisle & overpriced granola can do for a woman.

Being an energetic woman with a bit of ADD had me constantly searching for something to keep me busy. I didn't want to dissolve in front of the TV (though I do love a good episode of SWAT or NCIS). At first, I tried a few puzzles. The cats were not at all helpful in that arena. I bought several diamond-painting kits. That was fun... until it wasn't. Then I got some adult coloring books with colored pencils. I always loved coloring as a kid, however, the novelty wore off after a couple of weeks.

When I was 9, my stepmom taught me how to knit. I used to knit all the time. I especially liked making baby layettes, mainly because it didn't take forever to finish them. It was easy when I was younger, and my friends had new babies to make them for. I didn't just want to knit baby clothes with no baby in mind to receive it. I have yet to ever attempt an Afghan. I know I would never finish it. I did buy a bunch of yarn and started a scarf about 3 years ago. I am almost finished with it! I also won't knit when it's hot out. That is definitely a winter hobby for me. The thing that I found worked best was knitting washcloths. Easy patterns, and I could finish one pretty quickly. I made quite a few and gave them as gifts. I also make these little bristly ones that are amazing little scrubbies for cast iron pans or cooking stones. I still make them in the winter months, though it no longer feels like a thing I have

34

to do to keep busy. I now enjoy knitting again.

I also got really good at mowing the lawn and learning to use the weed-whacker. I still today hate using the weed-whacker. The first few months using it, something flew in my eye, and I had to go see the Ophthalmologist. He was pretty hard on me, making me feel like an idiot for not wearing protective glasses. My reaction: "I am so sorry my husband died and left me with this God-forsaken job to do! I never saw him wear protective eyewear when he did this, so I didn't know that was a thing!" He immediately apologized. I could tell he felt really bad, which *was* my goal. The first rule in doctoring is to never assume!!

I got myself a battery-operated, zero-turn lawnmower. It was daunting at first, and now I love it. The thought of dealing with a tractor that needs gas and oil and all that was completely overwhelming. Mowing the pastures is very meditative to me. I put in my earbuds and jam out, mostly to classic rock (70s, 80s, 90s). Music really helped me put the pep back in my step.

I remember how at first, I kept looking back at who I was before I met Bennie—like that was who I was going to be again now. Big Mistake. I was getting lost in figuring out what to do, how to support the kids, how to navigate this unexpected turn, and why I wanted to buy everything I saw, thinking it would comfort me. I was lost and flailing.

Back to therapy I went. It was SO helpful to talk to someone who was not part of my everyday life. I could say anything to her, and it didn't offend her or hurt her feelings. I am a huge believer in asking for help and yet it was the hardest thing for me to do until I needed a ton of help to navigate this new path I was on. I realized people really do want to help; you just need to have the guts to ask.

Another thing I did for myself was regular chiropractic care, massage therapy, and going to the hair salon after years of doing my own hair. I was taking care of myself with the help of others that I trusted. I was slowly emerging from out of the darkness and into the light.

My biggest project that has been a huge blessing has been building a large, raised bed vegetable garden and a separate raised bed herb garden. I put every bottomless container together myself and filled them up with dirt (on top of this Georgia clay). I must admit that I do LOVE buying garden chachkas and birdhouses to add charm and whimsy to my gardens. My favorite addition is solar lights!

I can't tell you how many times I have asked myself over the last few years, *why didn't you pay more attention when Dad was gardening?* I also find myself wishing he were still here to help me. He would have loved teaching me all his gardening tricks.

I have learned to can my own tomatoes, make homemade pepper jelly, and I even created my own recipe for bread and butter pickles (though that took a whole summer of making pickles over and over again until I found just the right combination). I also dehydrate a lot of herbs, tomatoes, and peppers.

It feels like I have my dad's family around me when I am gardening and creating great tasting food from vegetables and herbs I grow. My Aunt Patti used to can enough things from her garden to last through the winter months in Michigan. I always wanted her to show me how she did all that when I was younger. Now I have taught myself, and I love to make fresh basil pesto and sun-dried tomatoes. I think of her often when I am canning jellies, peppers, and tomatoes.

I bought a battery-powered pressure washer and washed the top half of the driveway. I remember taking a video of what I had done to send to a friend of mine back home. I was SO proud of myself!! I don't think the driveway had been power-washed for 15 years.

Another big project I took on was painting all the "outside" doors a color called *Charleston Green*. It's a very dark green (almost black) color. I had no earthly idea how hard it was going to be to paint white doors a dark color. I called my friend Ed, who has owned his own painting business for many years, because I needed his advice before I tackled this big project. I didn't want to take the doors off the hinges and one of the doors had a bunch of windowpanes. I thought, why reinvent the wheel? Why not ask an expert? Ed was great! He walked me through it and gave me the confidence to do it. Of course, he can paint a door like this in about 5 minutes, whereas it took me several hours! In the end, the 3 doors looked SO great. I was incredibly proud of myself for sticking with it and finishing all 3, though I honestly thought it would be much harder than it ended up being. Funny how easily we can freak ourselves out and become so overwhelmed sometimes.

One of my most favorite things to do is travel. This was a bone of contention with Bennie and I because I don't like to go back to the same place twice unless it is truly amazing. Bennie liked to go where he knew; though, if it were up to him, he would always go back to the Wright Patterson Air Force Base Museum every time.

I was always the family trip planner, and we always had GREAT vacations. Our first trip together after Bennie died was after our oldest daughter's high school graduation. We had been talking about going to Spain to see his mom's family after Emma graduated. I was not up for a trip to Spain on my own, so I planned a trip to the Bahamas. I had gone several times before when I lived in Miami and it was always fun and reasonable, especially going out to Paradise Island. This felt safe and familiar even though I was breaking my number 1 rule.

I invited one of my best friends, MaryAnne, to go with us. She and I have been friends since elementary school and my kids call her Aunt MaryAnne. She is a soul sister to me. I had such huge expectations for this trip and set myself up for failure and disappointment. Don't get me wrong—it had some great moments, though mostly I felt like it was too soon to be celebrating like this. It had only been 7 months since Bennie had passed, and I didn't realize how emotional it would be to attempt this big trip. MaryAnne was a life saver. She and I always kept each other laughing, and when I was spent and crying, she held me tight and reassured me.

The next big hurdle when we got back was managing all the VA paperwork for Emma to go to college. Emma had applied to the University of Kentucky as soon as she started her senior year of high school. She received her acceptance letter in early September and never applied anywhere else. I will never forget when she got the acceptance letter. We were worried because it was only 3 weeks from the time she had applied. Emma and I were both crying for joy while Bennie looked at us like we were insane.

"What are you guys crying about? This is GOOD news!" He exclaimed.

She had her sights on Equine Science Management and never looked back. You never know how much you don't know until you send your first kid to college. That was another emotional rollercoaster with a lot of firsts. I was so excited for her and also scared to let go of her.

This time I called on another best friend, Melissa, who is also my cousin Bert's wife. She went with us and helped us get Emma moved in, unpacked, and settled in her dorm. Melissa and I planned to stop in Pigeon Forge afterwards for a night so we could try to have some fun and lessen the emotional weight of sending my first-born baby off to college. We went to Dolly Parton's Dixie Stampede and had a great evening. I tried to find someone that could get a message to Dolly that I wanted to meet up with her again for a quick reunion... no luck there. Then it was back home to Georgia to find a new normal with Emma 6 hours away at school.

Emma was the one who mainly helped take care of the horses with me. Now it was down to me and Ally. There used to be 4 of us taking care of the horses; and now we were 2, and I was feeling the heavy burden both financially and physically.

Ally was also worried as she approached her senior year of high school. She knew I couldn't manage everything alone. Tanya, my long-time friend, came to my rescue. She knew an attorney and his family that had recently bought a house on 12 acres with nice horse facilities, and they were looking for horses to keep at home. Win-win.

We shipped the horses to their house, about an hour away from where we live. We have visited them a few times, and they seem very happy there. The family is amazing. They are well taken care of and have a lot more property to roam on. It is hard to go visit them, yet it is also hard not seeing our horses in our own pastures even though I am so grateful for the relief of knowing they still have a great life with a great family.

Life without Bennie didn't stop. It just slowed into something so foreign, so unfamiliar. I kept our routines, held space for my girls, and tried to recreate stability inside a story that had been rewritten without warning. Time is a quiet invitation that doesn't rush. It waits.

Letting go of the horses was one of those bittersweet decisions that reminded me how much had changed. The pastures were quieter, the house more still, and our lives slowly settled into a new rhythm. I held everything together for the girls, for the home, and for the legacy Bennie and I built together.

Somewhere in that quiet, something stirred. A whisper of possibility... of curiosity... of me.

While I wasn't exactly chasing love again, I was finally ready to do something I hadn't done in years: say yes to myself.

Chapter 11
Reclaiming My Yes

From heartbreak to Hinge—rediscovering joy one awkward date at a time.

It started with a comment I never expected.

After a team meeting, my boss pulled me aside. "I see you're still wearing your wedding rings. It's been a year. Don't you think it's time to take them off and start dating?"

I froze. My rings weren't just for decoration. They were memories. I had worn them for so long, the groove in my finger took forever to fade after I finally removed them. Taking them off felt like erasing a part of myself I wasn't ready to say goodbye to.

I turned to Gina, a close friend who'd lost her first husband very young. Her advice was gentle and wise: trial runs. Remove the rings for an hour or two, then try a half-day. Let the timeline be my own. She helped me see that "ready" doesn't come on a schedule; it arrives through healing.

It took a couple of months and eventually I put my rings away for good. Not because I was ready to date, but because I was ready to reclaim myself. My yes wasn't about someone else. It was about me.

Almost two years after losing Bennie, I downloaded a dating app. I had met Bennie that way, so maybe lightning could strike twice. I was dismayed how the dating jungle had evolved. It was full of blurry photos, bios that read like tax forms, and enough "Hey" messages and winks to fill a sad poem. I felt like I had entered a reality show where the prize was enduring small talk with strangers who love craft beer and hate punctuation. Still, I gave it a shot. I built my profile and picked photos where I looked like me—real, honest, a little exhausted, but sparkly enough to suggest I hadn't totally given up.

First dates were... well... *varied.*

I had a lot of conversations, and I really hated having to play that game. I was careful what I would share and, when it came time to plan an actual date, I would usually back out. I wasn't ready.

Finally, I agreed to meet someone for lunch and some time at the gun range. My goal was to just get out of the house and have fun. I didn't want to idly sit at a restaurant for dinner and do the small talk thing. I wanted to do something fun. We had a good time, though that was destined to never work out. In my mind, I kept saying, *He is my crash dummy, my practice round. If I can survive this, maybe I can move forward.* Don't get me wrong—he was a nice guy! I just was not ready for anything romantic yet. I still felt like I was cheating on my husband.

The next date I went on was horrible. I showed up for dinner at a Thai restaurant and the man I was meeting looked much older than his profile pictures. I honestly felt like I was having dinner with my father. He kept bragging about his money and the new car he paid cash for, which was in the parking lot near the door. As we were talking, he jumped up and screamed, "GOD DAMMIT!!" in the middle of the restaurant. Everyone glared at him. He told me he thought a guy that parked next to him dinged his car. He ran out of the restaurant in a panic. I waited for him to come back in, where he then apologized and made his excuses. He paid for dinner and walked me out, telling me what a great time he had and wanted to show me his fancy new sports car. It took everything I had not to laugh. Did he honestly think there would ever be a 2nd date? NEXT.

I took myself off the dating apps. It was just too much. I hated it. The 3 different apps I tried were really all the same: lots of creeps and fake accounts. I would rather be alone the rest of my life than do that again.

Then came the market guy.

We met at the grocery store after Gina had to reschedule dinner with me due to a tragic A/C failure in her yoga studio. The restaurant she and I were planning to meet at was next to my favorite market, so it was a great time to stock up since I was there.

He seemed great—charming, chatty with a northern vibe, and very confident. We had several phone conversations, and he had an edge to him I couldn't quite pin down. I ignored my gut... I shouldn't have.

He took me to dinner. We talked a lot. It was fine. He was very intrigued by my story of meeting Dolly Parton and really wanted to help me get reunited with her. The silver lining on this encounter was that some of his ideas on how to create a social media presence, "tell the world" my story, and knock on every door wasn't wrong.

Then he walked me to my car, and he extended his hand and said, "Give me your hand."

Sweet, right?

Except that he took my hand and placed it on his crotch. "I think it's amazing that a 60-year-old man can get an erection like this, don't you?" He asked.

OMG!! I was stunned... speechless. Seriously?? *Holy crap! Why me, Lord?!*

That was it. No more ignoring instincts. No more entertaining red flags just because I'd had a quiet month.

My sanctuary became a weekend with my soul sisters. Camilla, MaryAnne, and I had a fabulous weekend together doing a whole lot of nothing. Melissa came by and we ate, played games, and we laughed until we cried. We did face masks at night (which mine almost burnt my face off), soaked in the hot tub out back, sat in the sun and watched the dogs play, and roasted the world over stories and sarcasm.

These women—my girlfriends—they are my lifeline. They are precious, powerful, and one-of-a-kind. I've collected them over time, held them close, and leaned on them without shame.

I may not have found love again (yet), but I found something even better: proof that laughter, connection, and self-respect are still mine. And that's more than enough.

Chapter 12
The Dream I Almost Forgot
Reclaiming a spark that I buried beneath survival.

One night in 2011, I shot out of bed at 2am, wide awake and lit up by a dream. I ran into my home office, grabbed some paper, and started writing. I poured out pages of a story, complete with sketches. My imagination couldn't wait for morning. I had to catch every detail before it slipped away.

That night *Cowgirl Cassidy* was born: a children's book series about a horse-crazy girl growing up in Michigan, *my* Michigan. I could see the entire world in my head—five books full of adventure, heart, and humor.

My good friend Carolyn introduced me to Mary, a talented artist, and together we began to bring Cassidy to life. We spent hours brainstorming over pastries at Georgia's French Bakery, trying to translate Mary's rich paintings into illustrations fit for print. Neither of us had done this before and, while we were floundering, the passion was real. Mary and I became fast friends.

Then life got loud.

Work. Marriage. Motherhood. Loss. Farm life. Grief. Survival.

Fast-forward to 2025. I'm building my vision board and staring at *Cowgirl Cassidy* again. She's still kicking around in my heart, asking, "When are you coming back for me?"

I realized the harsh truth: I wasn't making time for her. I kept waiting for the perfect moment, the empty calendar, the clean desk. Someday wasn't a day on the calendar. **Someday is today.**

I found this quote for my Vision Board that spoke to my core: "Creativity is inventing, experimenting, growing, taking risks, breaking rules, making mistakes, and having fun." I found the theme for my board and my life! As Nike would say, "Just Do It!"

I gave up all my excuses around time and decided to make the time. Chocolate or Vanilla, choose. When you choose a dream with your whole heart, the universe either throws boulders or opens magical doors. No boulders *this* time.

I enrolled in a children's book writing course with Miriam Landry. Then I joined a Facebook group that Landry created for writers and illustrators. That's where I found Jill. The moment I saw her website, I just knew in my gut she was the one.

I reached out. Instant chemistry. And now, we're on track to publish Book One in early 2026.

The dream is breathing again.

I had to make so many unexpected changes in my life after Bennie died. I was so overwhelmed with all the things it takes to keep a small farm running. I am so incredibly thankful for my neighbors, Tom and Alice, who have taught me so much. They are in their 80s and the kindest people you could ever know. Tom saved me more times that I can remember over these past several years.

He scooped a dead squirrel out of my water trough. He showed me how to drive my truck back up to the barn to offload bales of hay and horse feed. When my yard looked like an inground sprinkler went off, he knew how to turn off the water by the edge of the property and set me up to have the water leak fixed. He has taught me how to survive farm life with skill, dignity, courage, and confidence.

Then there was the opossum incident.

I was mowing. I spotted something that looked like a terrified, lifeless Flat Stanley in my side yard. I yelled, "Holy shit! What is that?!"

It took me *days* to muster the courage to deal with it. When I finally did, I grabbed a rake, scooped up the opossum (which was not easy!), walked over to the fence by the easement, and tossed it into the woods... only for it to *bounce off a branch and ricochet back at me.*

I screamed into the void, "NOOOOO!!"

Why didn't I just call Tom?

I am proud to say that my Flat Stanley Opossum found his forever home in the woods... eventually. Did I scream? Yes. Did I curse my husband in the air for leaving me with this shit to deal with? Yes. Did I figure it out alone? Yes. Did

43

I have to figure it out alone? No. I chose to figure it out alone. Knowing I could do it without asking for help was worth the struggle.

That moment changed something. It wasn't just about rodents; it was about realizing that I'm capable of more than I thought, even when it's gross and unfair and a little comedic.

I've stopped telling myself the story that "I don't have time." The truth? I have time for what matters. I'm creating a home that's *my* home, not just the house we shared. I have two daughters in college and I'm no longer just surviving. I am living. No more keeping dusty relics around out of guilt. Now, it's only things I love that bring me joy.

I am happy that the girls still come home on their breaks and ask me to make their favorite foods. I love it when they call me to tell me all the things going on in their lives at school. The difference is that now I no longer *need* them to come back home to help me. I've rebuilt, reorganized, redesigned—and I've stayed in the family home I fought to keep.

How did I let all the time I used to dedicate to taking care of the horses just get filled in? I couldn't even put into words or thoughts how I used to manage so much more. I told myself a story that I don't have enough time, and the universe listened and delivered all kinds of fillers to me.

This is the year that I am creating a life for myself that I haven't yet imagined. No more limits. No more excuses. No more projects on the back burner.

At the end of 2024, I discovered Mel Robbins, and her book *Let Them* which turned the lights back on inside me. Her theory is simple and liberating: stop trying to control what people think. *Let them.* Stop shrinking. Stop apologizing. *Let Them* and *Let Me.*

Her podcasts have introduced me to so many amazing people, and I've absorbed new wisdom like a sponge. I'm not resurrecting the old Jolene. She's gone. I'm building a new one, day by day, voice by voice, dream by dusty dream.

And one of those long-shelved dreams? Seeing Dolly Parton again, for a long-overdue reunion.

Chapter 13
The Reunion that Time Forgot
The girl behind the name returns to find the songbird.

"I remember this little red-headed girl, green eyes, prettiest little thing... and I said, 'Well, what's your name?'
She said, 'Jolene.'
And I said, 'Well, I love that name.'
All the way back to the bus I'm going, 'Jolene, Jolene, Jolene...' so I wouldn't forget it.
— Dolly Parton, CBS Sunday Morning interview

Once Terri and I had come to terms with the fact that it really was that concert in Battle Creek where we met Dolly Parton that gave birth to the song *Jolene*, we were on a mission to reconnect. My sister was much more enthusiastic about this as she was and is truly a huge country music fan. I like a lot of types of music, including a lot of country music, though my #1 is classic rock n' roll. My sister has gone to many country music concerts throughout the years and always tried to talk to anyone that would listen in hopes of making a connection that would get us back to someone in Dolly's camp.

Surely, Dolly would want to have this reunion with that little girl that is now a woman... right?

45

Then came a call from Terri. "Send me a picture of your driver's license!" She had to be kidding. I asked her why. She proceeded to tell me she was going to a Dolly Parton concert, and she was bound to find someone who could get the information to Dolly about me.

"I really don't think it's necessary to take a copy of my driver's license, is it?"

She convinced me that this was the only way to prove that I am who I say I am, so I sent it to her. After the concert, she called and told me she found a security guard that was excited to help her pass the information along. I was having visions of this guy having a lot of my personal information in his hands... *yikes*!

Crickets.

Over the years, we have both sent letters and tried to make phone calls. Anytime we have been anywhere near Dollywood, we would look for someone who knows someone who knows Dolly that can help us reconnect.

I have used Instagram multiple times, sending messages to hundreds of different people, including Dolly's IG, hoping for a connection. I think I have sent the Jimmy Fallon show 25 different messages in the last few months.

Crickets.

We would go through phases where we would make huge efforts and then when nothing worked out we'd put it off to the side. We have both had tons of people who say they want to help us when they hear our story.

Still... crickets.

This year, 2025, something changed for me. When I heard the news of Carl Dean's passing, it was like a bell ringing for love gone quiet. Bennie's absence echoed beside it, reminding me that long stories deserve their last chapters.

Remember that thing I said in the beginning of Chapter 12: **Someday is today**. That is all I could think about. Those thoughts that *someday* we will figure out how to see Dolly again and have a reunion and trusting the universe to work it out for me were done.

Today is the day. This is the year.

I went into high gear, and my friend Carolyn told me that I should be shouting my story from the rooftop until someone listens. Others told me to use social media. Just get the word out! I created a few TikToks and some posts on Instagram and Facebook. Then I created a website to tell my story: www. theoriginalJolene.com. I put it all out on Facebook and Instagram, made my story and my page public, and just kept sharing.

I reached out to all the country music journalists I could find to see if they could give me bigger outreach. Some responded, others not at all. Some were mildly interested and were hesitant as I didn't have a picture of me with Dolly at that concert in 1971. I don't think they realize how bulky cameras were in 1971 and that really wasn't something you did back then. We didn't take pictures of everything we did and everything we ate back then.

I just know in my heart that if Dolly heard my story, she would remember me and the details of our meeting. I had heard her say in an interview once that some people have tried to tell her they were that little girl she met, and she said that only that Jolene would know the details that would tell her that *she* is the one.

I was always hesitant to share certain details after I heard that. I wanted to keep those all to myself so no one would impersonate me. Not anymore. It's time to shout it all from the rooftops and make some noise.

I am Jolene... Hear me roar!

When I went back to Michigan for two weeks at the beginning of June (2025), I had breakfast with my good friend from school, Kari. I told her my story. She was so surprised that I had not told her before that day. I have known Kari since 7th grade. I told her all the whys, and she told me she wanted to help me in any way she could.

Kari delivered in spades.

She connected me with Anita Cochran, who she knows because their kids were both at UofM together and Anita is also from Michigan originally. I told Anita my story and she thought it was amazing and passed along my information to some people she thought could get the word to Dolly.

I was filled with the energy from those who were hearing my story for the first time—everyone cheering me on and praying for a successful connection.

Then in July, when I was driving home from South Carolina from my Goddaughter's house, Kari called me. "You haven't answered my text yet!?" Of course, I had not seen her text since I was driving. She proceeded to tell me what it was about. She was bursting with excitement.

She sent me a link where Dolly Parton is looking for "concert stories" from her fans to spotlight in her new book. She was reading to me what Dolly is looking for, and she is yelling, "YOUR STORY IS *THE* STORY!"

I was dead tired before Kari called me, hoping to make it home without falling asleep at the wheel. I got home and was filled with energy as I clicked on the link she had sent me. Two submissions were being accepted: an audio clip and a video clip. I did a practice run, filled out the form, and then recorded an audio clip. I ended up submitting the practice run. The audio clip was under 2 minutes (as required) and I thought it sounded good. If it ain't broke, don't fix it.

The next morning, I recorded the video clip and included a picture of myself before that concert as well as a picture of my sister at that age. I hit "submit".

My voice now carries through the ether. Could Dolly's ears be next? The chorus of silence may finally break. And if the universe is listening, I hope it's humming "Jolene."

Grandma's & Dad's Recipes

GRANDMAS DRESSING

PUT 2/3 of A loaf of Bread on A cookie
SHEET IN YOUR OVEN OVER Nite (oven off)
Dice 3 STALKS of CeleRy ANd cook foR
15 min — cuT DRy Bread IN To cubes
PLAce IN LARGe Bowl Add:

(1) 1 small onion - diced
(2) The Cooked celeRy
(3) 2 Tbs chopped PARsley
(4) 2 Tbs dRy SAge
(5) 1 Tsp SAlt
(6) 1/2 Tsp PeppeR

Now dRizzel 1/4 cup sAlad oil oveR
STuffing ANd mix well. moisTeN DRessing
w/ A smAll AmT of The wATeR The celeRy
wAs cooked IN — AbouT 1/2 cup — do
noT mAke To weT — DRessing will geT
wetteR As it cooks

EGG Noodles

(1) COMBiNE 1 CUP All PURPOSE FLOUR
AND ½ TSP of SALT IN A Bowl

(2) Lightly BeaT one EGG ANd Pour
INTo FLOUR

(3) MiX uNTil Dough FORMS BAll, if
Dough is To dRy Add 1 oR 2 Tbs of
WATER

(4) Dough will be veRy CRumbly donT be
CONCEARNed — FLATEN BAll — And
WRAP w/ Plastic WRAP — RefRigeRATe
FoR oNe HOUR — NOW The Dough will
veRy Elastic

(5) CUT BAll iNTO 4 Pieces FLATEN
The Pieces And Roll ouT oN A
Lightly FLOURed Bond

(6) Roll up Thin Slices of Dough And
slice w A KNife

(7) UNRoll eACH noodle AS SOON AS you
CUT iT oR it will sTick To giETheR

(8) LAy noodles ouT To DRy oN Towels
ABOUT 1 hR.

Polish Sausage w/ Kraut

I used to put every thing in a
pot and boil it until the potatoes
were done. But I have since
learned that roasted sausage
taste better then boiled, so this
is how I make it now:

cut Polish Sausage in to serving
size pieces - prick ea piece
4 or 5 times with a knife
place in single layer in a shallow
baking dish - bake in pre heated
300° oven for 25 - 30 min until
nicely browned.
Now about the Kraut - do not use
canned Kraut - it is mushy. Fresh
is much better. Fresh Kraut is the
Kraut that comes in a plastic bag
in the refrigerated section of store.

Peel Potatoes (Idaho are Best) and cut in halve place in bottom of pan.

(1) Now there are 2 ways to prepare the kraut: If you like a strong tasting kraut — simply drain the juice off the kraut and place the drained kraut on top the potatoes

(2) If you like a milder tasting kraut drain the juice from the kraut and put the kraut in a pan of cold water — rinse it around some and drain it again — now put it on top of the potatoes add salt + pepper to taste — fill the pan with enough water to barley cover the kraut bring to a boil reduce to a simmer and cook partialy covered for 30 — 35 min or until potatoes are tender.

RHINOCEROUS MEAT

IN THIS DISH THE KEY IS THE TECHNIQUE AND EACH STEP IS CRITICAL:

1. 3 TO 4 LB. CHUCK ROAST (FROM FRONT SHOULDER OF COW) CUT SEVERAL SLITS IN THE ROAST SLICE ABOUT 4 CLOVES OF GARLIC INSERT THE SLICES INTO THE SLITS SALT AND PEPPER THE ROAST ON BOTH SIDES. TO MAKE THIS DISH YOU MUST HAVE A DUTCH OVEN WHICH IS LIKE A 6" DEEP HEAVY SKILLET

2. PUT ABOUT 1/2" OF OIL IN THE D. OVEN OVER HIGH HEAT. BROWN THE ROAST ON BOTH SIDES ABOUT 15 MIN THIS IS CRITICAL STEP AS THE BROWING SEALS IN THE JUICES AND THE JUICES THAT STICK TO THE BOTTOM OF THE PAN MAKES THE GRAVY

Remove ROAST FROM PAN AND POUR off
All but one Tbs of GReaSe ReTURN
meat To PAN And Add WATER Almost
To ToP of ROAST. BRing To A Boil
Reduce Heat To SLow Simmer COVER
AND COOK I HR. if WATER EVApoRATes
To much Add more Boiling WATER
At End of Hour Add POTATOES CUT
IN HAlve CARROTS cut IN HAlve AN
ONiON cut IN quARTERS COVER And
Simmer 1 To 1½ HRS LONGER
Remove meaT And Veggies To A
PlAtter And Place in A WARM OVEN
200° Add enough WATER To PAN
So That you HAve 2 To 3 cups of Juices.
Add one LARge Tbs of FLOUR AND ONE TBS
CORN STARCH To A small dish mix well
SLOwly Add 2/3 cup of cold WATER
To FORM A SLURy BRING PAN Juices
To A SLow Boil SLowly Add SLURY
WHile STIRRing And cooking UNTil gRAVy
Reachs desired Thickness. If GRAVy
is NOT DARK enough you cAN Add one
oR Two Beef Bullion cubes

Add 1 Bay Leaf + ¼ Tsp Thyme

The END

55

www.ingramcontent.com/pod-product-compliance
Lightning Source LLC
Chambersburg PA
CBHW020810130626
46554CB00006B/2364